First Printing: 2015

ISBN 978-1508582007

Lisa Harrison

POMO Creative

PO Box 4750

Sunshine Coast Mail Centre 4560

Australia

www.pomo.com.au

www.lisaharrison.com.au

Contents

Welcome

This book is the sixth in a series of books published in 2014-15; a complete guide to the world of social media for business.

The first book gave you the basics setting up your digital footprint. The second focused on how to build and maintain your social networks and relationships. The third covered e-marketing as an essential part of your online strategy. Books four and five addressed managing websites and setting up your customer standards.

If you are reading this series I know that for you it is important for your business to innovate and grow. This sixth volume takes a look at the process of assessing just what resources you need in order to be effective online, including their purchase, maintenance and use to improve your business.

I encourage you to do a stocktake of your business resources. You'll be surprised at how quickly some of those previously considered assets have turned into liabilities. That's why resource management is so important.

I hope you enjoy reading it and working through the activities.

I wish you good luck with mastering your website!

Lisa Harrison

Introduction

As HG Wells says, "Adapt or perish, now as ever, is Nature's inexorable imperative."

Is your business as efficient and effective as you would like it to be? Do you think it could perform more professionally, if only you had the time and resources to focus on getting it into better shape. I ask you, what cost will there be to your business if you don't invest those time and resources?

In my classes, I use the analogy that a successful social media profile is like going to the gym. If you attend the gym a couple of days a week you will see some results but not as quickly as those who attend 5 times a week in combination with a healthy diet and lifestyle. The same goes for your social media profile. If you spend more time online, using a strategy, as well as choosing the best resources, you will find you're your goals will be reached a lot quicker.

Successful businesses invest time in managing appropriate, innovative and effective business resources because it enables them to concentrate on improving profits and reducing costs.

Social media takes time and this is the most precious resource of all, as once it is gone it is gone. Be smart and efficient with the resources you have to achieve the results you need.

Getting the Most From This Book

This book takes a look at the foundations of your online presence. In other words, the practical resources you need to carry out your digital strategy.

Consistency and efficiency are key to effective social media for business and while you might get away with winging it for a while, sooner or later your online success will depend on having the appropriate resources and internal procedures for your digital communications.

From knowing what's available to assessing what you need, and from purchasing to maintenance, this book contains all you need to know to support your social media and wider digital strategy with the right resources for the job.

Although this is not a coursebook, the emphasis is very much on helping you to use the knowledge and techniques to create real and tangible business benefits. With that in mind, the contents are based on:

- **Global best practice** – incorporating concepts from a range of digital commentators and leading practitioners.

- **Practical application** – giving practical insights resourcing your social media activities. Throughout this book, I encourage you to take action in a planned and strategic manner.

What Lies Ahead...

I've split this book into three chapters to give you a structure which will take you through the key aspects of resourcing your online business in a clear and helpful fashion. To give you a road map for what you're about to read, here's a summary of the chapters:

Chapter 1: Determine Resource Requirements

Know what's available to you in the online world and compare that to the aims of your strategic business and operational plans to establish your online resource requirements.

Chapter 2: Acquire and Allocate Resources

It's not just about buying to match your needs, there are also implications about quality checking that somehow are easily forgotten online. Also, fair allocation of the resources, with appropriate staff and stakeholder involvement is critical to good management.

Chapter 3: Monitor and Report on Resource Usage

Knowing what you need and obtaining it is just the beginning. The real art of resource management comes from understanding how those resources are utilised and checking their ongoing effectiveness. Continuous improvement is key.

CHAPTER 1
Determine Resource Requirements

The first step in resourcing any activity is to work out exactly what you'll need. Which, in turn, requires you to know what it is you're attempting to achieve. This logic brings us back to your business and operational (and digital) plans.

Resourcing the Plan

Bearing in mind the various elements of a comprehensive digital marketing plan, the task of resourcing planned activities will involve multiple strands.

Developing your organisation's online marketing campaigns requires the right tools.

Determining the right tools for the job depends on the following factors:

- Location and access to technology.

- The industry your organisation operates in.

- The number of employees you have.

- Your target market and ideal client.

- The products and services you deliver.

It goes without saying that digital marketing requires access to a computer and a decent internet connection; i.e. dial-up just does not cut it (and yes, even just a year or so ago, figures showed more than a quarter of a million Australians were still dialling up to access the internet). However, this is the very minimum.

When developing the plan of how you will promote your organisation or brand, you need a basic awareness of the resources that are available to you.

The following tables contrast the varying needs of traditional and online marketing strategies.

Traditional Marketing And Paid Mass Communications

Type of marketing channel	Promotion options	Support tools available
Print media placement	• Print in periodicals • Paid print ads • Print inserts on boarding passes, tickets, hotel materials	• Accessories with printed logos • Newspaper coupons • Flyers • Inserts in periodicals • Print on public transport vehicles or in public places
TV/Radio placement	• Paid TV/radio • Infomercials • Show sponsorships • TV/Radio ad spots	• Reality TV • Sponsored documentary • Pre-roll ads at the movies • Telemarketing
Other mass media channels	• Outdoor advertising (billboards) • Cab/Bicycle branding • Human mascots • Sky banners	• Petrol station pump and counter advertising • Freestanding posters • Blimps • Skywriting
Product placement	• Product-themed or branded entertainment, games, movies, music, festivals, apps	• Product placement in games, movies, TV/radio programs, music, apps

Digital Marketing

Type of marketing channel	Promotion options	Support tools available
Corporate presence and its components	• Website • Blog • User community sites • Organic discovery through search engine optimisation	• Content sites • RSS feeds • Interactive demos or product previews • Interactive feedback collection
Third-party hosted online content	• Social media company profile pages • Social media personal profile pages (for managers) • Q&A sites • Community sites	• Online directories • Industry resource sites • Marketplace sites • Local search • Other online content channels • Video hosting sites
Desktop software-based channels	• Widgets and toolbars • Adware	• Apps
Code-based linkage to shareable content	• QR codes	• Geo-location services
Online media placement	• Pay Per Click (search engine, social media) • Paid display ads • Popups • In-text contextual • Google AdSense	• Online video ads • Paid listings • Paid directory listings • Paid premium listings • Paid mobile display ads • Paid microsites

Invest in Technology

Your digital marketing toolkit will be a work in progress as new devices are invented daily. A continuous improvement strategy is essential to maintain effective use of digital tools. However there are a few essentials that will be in practically constant use:

- Access to the internet – via either ADSL, 4G or cable.

- Hardware – computers, mobile and other devices, furniture, stationery, etc.

- Software – browser programs, word processing programs, design programs, apps, widgets, etc.

- Online subscriptions – blogs, news publications, social media aggregators, etc.

- Education and training – professional qualifications, workplace inductions, OH&S, first aid, tailored training for specific workplace duties, etc.

Browser Programs

So you have a computer? Great. Next you'll need to access several different internet browsing programs (i.e. Firefox, Safari, Internet Explorer, Google Chrome, Opera, etc.) and, if possible, operating systems (i.e. Mac, Windows, Linux, etc). This is because target audiences don't all access the internet in the same way, so when web sites are created they need to be compatible for viewing in each of these browsers and operating systems.

Although the web developer who builds sites or apps or games is responsible for making these online products compatible with the majority of the market, marketers will still need to see and know what the end product looks like and its functionality.

Smartphones

More than half of the Australian population now owns a smartphone, according to research from the Australian Communications and Media Authority (ACMA) and this proportion is steadily growing. Australians (not to mention the rest of the global populace) access the internet on these devices not just daily, but multiple times a day.

With this in mind, marketers need to know how to use these devices and how to apply digital promotion campaigns to suit the needs and desires in the marketplace. In Australia, smartphones either use a Mac or Android operating system so if marketers can have access to both of these it's an advantage.

Tablet and Mobile Devices

This a growing sector in the world of computer technology. Again, websites need to be tailored to fit the specifications and functionality of these devices. Results vary, sometimes substantially, from how the site would look on a regular computer.

Tablet computers are touch screen, have in-built cameras and are easily portable meaning the way users interact with these devices is something that needs to be considered separately from other technologies.

Mobile Applications or 'Apps'

An app is a piece of software for smartphones, tablets or computers. This software is downloaded from the internet and can perform a multiplicity of functions – from practical-use apps, i.e. internet banking, to the utterly useless (but often entertaining).

Apps can be fun, competitive, add extra security to your device, etc. The types of apps digital marketers need to own and make use of currently include: Facebook and Facebook Pages (this is for tracking business profiles) apps, Twitter, LinkedIn, Google+, and Hootsuite or TweetDeck. The list is potentially infinite but the above represent a good start.

Social Media Tools

As discussed in earlier books, the term 'social media' encompasses a wide variety of platforms. To gauge which ones you need to concentrate on let's have a look at the market share as at March 2013.

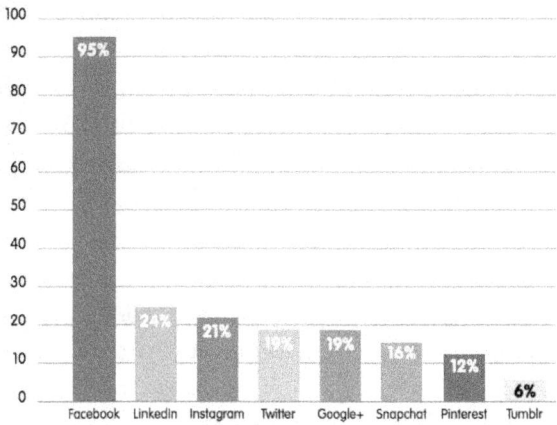

Social Media Use in Australia March 2013 - source: Sensis Social Media Report 2014.

As we can see, larger sites like Facebook, Twitter, LinkedIn, Instagram and blogging platforms are driving much of the engagement.

EXAMPLE – Facebook users

Facebook remains the most-used social networking platform, as two-thirds of online adults say that they are Facebook users. Women are more likely than men to be Facebook users, and Facebook use is especially common among younger adults.

Social media sites used by gender and age

Social media sites used	Male	Female	14-19	20-29	30-39	40-49	50-64	65+
Facebook	93%	96%	94%	95%	94%	92%	97%	100%
LinkedIn	28%	21%	0%	28%	30%	33%	26%	14%
Instagram	12%	30%	53%	31%	20%	15%	3%	3%
Twitter	25%	14%	15%	27%	23%	11%	22%	5%
Google+	21%	19%	27%	21%	21%	15%	16%	13%
Snapchat	12%	20%	61%	24%	4%	12%	0%	0%
Pinterest	6%	17%	6%	16%	12%	12%	15%	1%
Tumblr	4%	9%	24%	8%	1%	2%	5%	5%

Source: Sensis Social Media Report 2014.

So it's pretty obvious that Facebook dominates but YouTube is a hot contender, and of course it's advantageous to engage in Twitter. Beyond these, it's a decision that depends on what industry your organisation is in and where the target audience swims, which we discuss later in this book.

Aggregator Programs

Once you have established a number of social media profiles, you'll find that managing them all can be a logistical nightmare. For example, you have to log in to each account separately and respond to individual notifications here and there. Keeping up with new fans or followers or subscribers can consume your waking hours if you're not savvy. This is where aggregators come in.

These programs are designed to help you manage all of your social media profiles from one place so you can see all the activity of all of your social network profiles all in one screen. Examples of aggregators include Hootsuite, TweetDeck and Sprout Social. There are hundreds of aggregators on the market and they each have different functions and price tags. To find which aggregator will suit your needs, you may have to try a couple first. Most have free trial periods so make use of them!

Customer Resource Management – CRM

CRMs are essential for any form of marketing but in particular digital marketing. These programs are like digital filing cabinets filled with the contact details of customers (or potential customers), businesses and even employees associated with your business.

CRMs have many functions but are mainly used to assist with newsletter mail outs and data collection, i.e. who is on your mailing list for your newsletter but not one of your Facebook likers?

Examples of CRMs include Highrise and SalesForce.

Google Tools

Besides being a seemingly all-knowing internet search engine, Google has several other functions of use to those looking to market themselves and their companies online. These include:

- Google AdWords

- Google Docs

- Google Keyword Tool

- Google Alerts

- Google News

- Google Reader

- Google Places

Content Creation and Online Resources

Blogging and creating content relevant to your target audience and industry has several advantages for digital marketing purposes. For starters it builds traffic towards your website. The more traffic visiting your website, the more opportunities you create for sales. If you link your blog to your social media profiles this will procure even more traffic back to your website (we talk about how to do this later in the book).

Writing a blog about industry-specific information also positions you as a source of credibility and even an expert in your field. People are more likely to buy from someone they feel they 'know' and they are more likely to buy from someone who knows what they're talking about and can speak with some authority about their product or service. Blogs can be free or you can pay for pages with more functionality.

Online resources that will help readers access the content you are creating include RSS feeds and email alerts.

Gamification

Gamification is the creation and implementation of games in non-gaming environments in order to engage users, access customer feedback and maintain client loyalty.

> EXAMPLE – Yahoo!7
>
> Australian broadcast and online media partnership Yahoo!7 launched its Fango mobile app in November 2011. This mobile app allowed TV viewers to interact with shows via gamification techniques like checking-in and earning badges. By December 2014, the organisation was moving to wrap Fango up as part of the more recent Plus7 app, but in that three-year period, Fango was downloaded more than a million times. This kind of success is achieved by the combined marketing, customer service and web development arms of an organisation with the intention of maximising customer engagement and fascination with the brand.

Education

Another important workplace resource is education and making further learning available. Provision of education and training leads to better understanding and performance of work practices. In the case of digital marketing and the social media sphere, new ideas, approaches and trends develop daily.

To keep-up-to-date with these innovations, staff should be allowed time each week or month to read up on new technologies, watch appropriate webinars and even share what they know with others in the workplace.

Formal accredited training is also very important to maintain staff skills and efficiency.

What this costs the organisation, who attends this training, where it is held and when it is due for reassessment are all important pieces of information that need to be noted and understood by the organisation. The purpose of keeping these records is to ensure staff are educated in relevant areas of expertise with notifications when this training is out of date and due for review.

Involve Others in Identifying Your Resource Requirements

Now that you have determined what resources your organisation can access to market itself in the digital realm, it's time to identify which of these resources your organisation requires and it helps to get this information straight from the horse's mouth – your employees.

This is important because, although some resources will be standard across the organisation i.e. computers and internet access, other resources, like programs and applications, will only be needed by some departments. For example – will your organisation allow all employees to access Facebook, Twitter and YouTube at work, or will this remain the domain of the marketing department?

Education and training are an essential part of any business, and as technology changes and develops so must an organisations training programs. Organisations must keep up to date with technology and accredited training so that employees remain up to date with industry trends and expectations of consumers.

The key is to provide genuine opportunities for staff suggestions. But encouraging staff to contribute their ideas and opinions is not as simple as offering a feedback box and waiting for the suggestions to start flying in. To receive ideas that can make a difference, management needs to take the first step.

Employees will not bother giving any ideas if they do not feel anything will come of them. Management needs to follow up on ideas and tell the individuals and workgroups how their idea fare/ed. Taking the suggestions seriously means that more serious contributions will be offered.

Workplace Communication Channels

In order to get the ball rolling, there are a number of ways any organisation can successfully extract the right information regarding workplace needs:

Staff Intranet

This is an option for larger organisations where access to a staff intranet is standard. Put simply, a staff intranet is a computing system designed to allow employees across an entire company to have access to a central portal for workplace resources like OH&S guidelines and forms, important updates on new information and news, etc. The organisation can provide a feedback submission section on this intranet and even make it anonymous. Management could offer some kind of reward scheme for the best suggestions to spur activity.

Staff Meetings

Staff meetings are commonplace in any organisation and are often a great place to receive information about workplace operations from staff directly. To make sure the right information is offered up, management can choose to mix up the meeting's agenda or hold a separate meeting altogether to find out about workplace equipment and resources. By changing the circumstances around the meeting, management is indicating that the session is important and needs employee's attention.

Brainstorming Sessions

Brainstorming during a staff meeting is a quick way to collect ideas and can help staff be more creative and inventive with their answers. This activity can be conducted in a number of ways but basically involves each person in the room offering a word or phrase around a central idea. These words are displayed on a white board or smart board for all to see. Seeing other answers can spark ideas for new words, particularly when the personalities and experience histories of the people in the session are mixed.

Group Pages, such as Facebook or LinkedIn Groups

Another way to connect staff with a passage to information sharing is to create a group in Facebook. This requires staff to have an account on the platform and access this at work. But once set up, it can be totally private so that only the members of the group can see it. Then those members can add comments, suggestions and pictures and also support each other's ideas and like posts they agree with. It is also a good place to foster a feeling of community within the workplace.

External Advice

Sometimes organisations need to consult experts outside of the business about resource requirements. Whether these external parties be regulatory bodies, industry associations, government agencies, business advisers or financial institutions, making the decision to go outside the business for advice must come from management.

The information garnered from these sources may include: regulations and standards around advertising certain products and services, laws pertaining to your industry, approvals, advice about web development and/or acquiring specialised programs.

Ensure expenditure is realistic

Once you've consulted the relevant parties and established the resources you need, the next step is to work out how much these will cost.

In the case of social media marketing, the majority of these resources cost nothing at all. It's free to access Facebook, start up a Twitter account or list your business in Google Places. The real cost is time.

It takes time to position a business page in Facebook as desirable, it takes time to build your army on Twitter, and it takes time to scout out connections and collect recommendations on LinkedIn. To establish how much time to allocate to social media activities you need to look at the return on investment (ROI) you receive from these platforms.

ROI

Measuring the success of a social media campaign is a two-step process:

- Firstly, you need to define exactly what you intend to achieve with the campaign. Don't just look at the number of likers you've garnered or the number of retweets you've scored with your content, you need to look at what those numbers have led to. Have you seen more traffic flow to your website? More sales via online ordering systems? Or more money per sale online?

- Once you've got an idea of what you set out to achieve, you then need to collect data to prove whether social media marketing has contributed to your goals. You can find all the data you need through the use of Google Analytics, Facebook Insights, and aggregators which will tell you how much traffic you are getting, who's engaged by your campaigning, where traffic to your sites comes from, how long visitors spend on your sites and what the 'hot spots' on your pages are.

Another ROI indicator that is easily measured is Facebook's e-commerce application. This allows business page visitors to view and purchase products straight from the business's profile. The business page administrator is offered clear figures on how many sales are garnered via Facebook.

Mobile applications are making it possible to measure fresh angles on social media ROI. Apps that allow users to check-in at specific locations and redeem digital coupons in the process like Foursquare all make measuring the ROI on social media easier and more tangible because these numbers are delivered straight to the organisation.

How to calculate the ROI of specific campaigns will be discussed later in this book in Chapter 3.

Word of Mouth – The Greatest Reward

All of the above are tangible examples of how to determine the level of expenditure businesses should outlay on social media marketing campaigns, however the greatest ROI organisations can hope to gain from investing in social media activity is word-of-mouth (WoM) referrals, which is not so easily measured.

WoM is marketing gold as it leads to trust from the marketplace and subsequent new fans that want what their friends are experiencing. Social media marketing can be considered the lowest-cost method to acquire new customers due to the power of WoM.

This is done with targeted posts and content which is then spread throughout the organisation's network of followers in the hope that friends of friends of friends will share, like, retweet, pin etc.

The Price Tag on Social Media Marketing

It would be a myth to say an organisation won't need to fork out a cent (besides wages) to establish a strong social media presence. There are essential resources that carry price tags and, as with any other part of the business, it pays to do the research and shop around.

What's Worth Paying For and What Isn't?

Access to a computer and the internet is essential for social media marketing. There is an initial cost for the computer, you may choose to also purchase warranties to save on maintenance fees. Then you'll need to purchase the programs you intend to use (i.e. Word, InDesign etc). There is also a price tag on security programs to protect your data.

Another cost involved may be the equipment and set up for an in-house server. You should also look at purchasing extra digital storage space and even programs intended to make filing and archiving as efficient as possible.

Then there's the cost of monthly internet connection and phone lines - the list goes on...

As far as the extra devices you need, it's a matter of looking at your target audience and what they use. As an example, if your target market is a consumer living in regional Australia between the ages of 35 and 50, it is less likely they would be using tablet computers to access the internet or even smart phones. It is far more likely they would be using the internet infrequently from a regular desktop set up. In this case you would not need to cater to the latest 4G phone or Apple touchscreen watch.

Another resource digital marketers may need to pay for is aggregators. Although some of these are free to use, i.e. HootSuite and TweetDeck, they're limited to looking after only a small number of accounts and they only offer the minimum of functions. Other aggregators that are paid programs like Sprout Social are better equipped to deal with a large amount of traffic, accounts and scheduled posts. They also offer great social media metrics and the opportunity for several users to access information and flag information for co-workers.

Whether an organisation chooses to pay or just access a free aggregator program depends on the needs of the organisation and how much social media activity it intends to engage in. Whoever makes the final decision should always have an eye on the future. Does the business intend to grow its social media presence/activity? Does it intend to limit its activity to only Facebook and YouTube? Planning for change is important and will save money down the line.

Paying for Online Advertising

Pay Per Click – PPC is a type of online advertising where the advertiser only pays if their ad is clicked by a visitor who then arrives at a preselected destination, i.e. usually a website landing page. You'll find PPC advertising at the top of your Google search and even in your Facebook news feed. How to sculpt a PPC campaign, what it should achieve and how much it will cost is usually dictated by the advertiser.

So a click on the ad can cost as little as 1 cent to the advertiser however PPC is usually an auction where other advertisers are also vying for attention from the same target market. The advertisers who bid more money will appear more prominently then those who choose to bid less per click.

Facebook Advertising – Facebook offers a variety of advertising options and can be targeted to specific age groups, interest groups, geographic locations, etc.

Facebook Ads are to the right of the Facebook screen and are standard advertisements like you would see on other web pages. Users can like these ads if they choose to. They appear in simple ad form with the point of sending the user to an external page, or a Facebook business page.

Sponsored stories appear as posts in users news feeds when someone interacts with a promotion. So when you see "John Smith likes Shop X" that is a sponsored story that Shop X have paid to generate. These stories appear in the user's friends' news feeds so the potential reach is extensive.

Promoted posts are a regular post you put into the Facebook status bar but you pay for these status posts to come at the top of your followers' news feeds. Promoted posts cannot have more than 20 per cent text in them so they're best left for pictures.

Event sponsorship is similar to paying for a promoted post but instead you pay to promote an event. Here you can increase the attendance of your event by tailoring the ad to only show up to people who are likely to be interested in the event.

Google AdWords – Google AdWords is an easy way to advertise online and is mentioned earlier in this book. It offers pay-per-click advertising, cost-per-thousand-impressions advertising, and site-targeted advertising for text, banner, or rich-media adverts. Any time a user searches Google, a number of results show up in a yellow banner at the very top of the list. Nowadays however, most users know that these links are Google AdWords advertisements and they may skip them for the organic results.

Paying for a Professional – Quite often companies need to outsource all or part of their marketing promotions and digital marketing is no different. The decision to outsource this sort of work comes down to weighing up whether it could be done in-house, whether a new position needs to be created and a new person hired in the organisation or whether it's best to pay an external party to conduct the work. Of course a major determinant is budget, however the cost of paying a professional to do specialised work that will benefit the business should never be the sole deciding factor.

As discussed earlier in this section, time is a major digital marketing cost as well. When a company pays an external party to perform digital marketing activities (or any other extra business functions) on its behalf, this frees-up time for the business operators to focus on performing their regular day-to-day operations.

Putting the Case for Resources

There are a number of ways to report what tools, resources or advice an organisation needs to address shortfalls. Small businesses may have an informal 'tell the boss' process, while larger companies generally require communication to go through several channels before a purchase for the business can take place. Some organisations may have specific forms or a workplace resourcing or procurement policy.

Reports might be given verbally on a regular basis at staff meetings or done up as processed written reports resulting from extended research.

When recommending resources for an organisation's social media and digital marketing activities, it might sometimes be necessary to draft a persuasive report.

This may be the case where:

- A large outlay of money is required.

- Targeted training needs to be conducted with many individuals.

- Many workstations or devices need to be updated.

- Work roles/conditions will be affected, etc.

Constructing a Written Report

In communicating when business resources are needed, you need to take into account the audience – who's receiving the report? Do they know much about this department? Are they familiar with the specific technical language being used? Some areas of social media and digital marketing are quite complex and may require extra explanation.

The format, style and structure of a resource recommendations report follows a standard formula:

Terms of reference – This section gives all of the background information on the reason the report has been written and submitted. It usually includes the names of who has written the report or who has requested it be investigated and submitted.

Procedure – The procedure explains the exact steps taken and methods used to establish the findings. This may include the exact questions asked in a staff feedback survey or precisely which devices were tested and how, etc.

    EXAMPLE

    A representative selection of 15% of the client base was surveyed online using Survey Monkey in the period between April 1 and April 15.

    The following questions were posed:

- Have you visited Shop X's Facebook page? – Y / N

- If so, have you 'liked' Shop X's Facebook page? – Y / N

- Why/Why not? – written answer

- Did you know you can make purchases on Shop X's Facebook page? – Y / N

- Have you made any purchases via Shop X's Facebook page?

Findings – The findings section is about identifying what discoveries have been made during the course of the report investigation. This section needs to include tables, graphs and other statistics where possible.

EXAMPLE

55% of the client base had visited Shop X's Facebook page and 96% of these respondents had 'liked' it.

Most respondents cited their reason for 'liking' the page was to find out about deals and special offers from Shop X.

Those respondents who had visited the page but not 'liked' it cited not wanting Shop X posts in their news feeds.

The 60% of respondents who had not visited and/or 'liked' Shop X's Facebook page cited several reasons: 50% did not know Shop X had a Facebook page

25% (30% of the overall respondents) do not have a Facebook account, 8% do not have internet and 17% did not complete the survey.

Only 20% of Shop X's existing Facebook fans knew about the e-commerce function on Shop X's Facebook page.

Of this 20% only 4% had made a transaction using this function.

Recommendations – The recommendations state the resources, activities, and/or changes the writer of the report has identified as needed, based on the findings. It should specifically outline why these actions are recommended, i.e. due to low cost, safety risk, loss of clientele or staff, etc. This section also needs to list the recommendations on a highest to lowest priority basis and outline deadlines and time frames.

EXAMPLE

The following recommendations have been ordered in priority of when the actions need to be taken.

1. One in three clients do not know Shop X is on Facebook so promotional material and the website must direct all clients to the Facebook page to boost awareness.

Time frame for this action: before end of May.

2. Collect ideas from Marketing Department staff on how to educate users about using Facebook for business so as to allow them to 'like' Shop X's page but select to not have all Shop X posts appear in their news feed. This will hopefully overcome a major barrier to users 'liking' Shop X.

Time frame for this action: before end of May.

3. Discuss the possibility of creating a special offer or competition for users to like Shop X's Facebook page.

Time frame for this action: before end June.

4. Meet with senior management to discuss budget for Facebook advertising to direct fans and non-fans to the e-commerce function on Shop X's profile.

Time frame for this action: before end June.

Why Identifying Resource Requirements is So Important

Determining which resources are necessary requires a strict focus on the target audience. You must establish what devices, social media platforms and publications your customers make use of and then include these in your organisation's marketing mix to place your product/service/brand in front of your audience. Educating your staff about the use of these resources is necessary to maintain workplace efficiency and avoid mistakes. Keeping your employees training up to date means not only will they perform their job better but they will know what resources they need in order to continue doing the work they do.

END OF CHAPTER ACTIVITY – Determine Resource Requirements

1. What recommendations would you make on activities for the business with regards to social media and digital marketing, including:

    *   hardware

    *   software

    *   online subscriptions

    *   allocation of time by individuals

    *   education and training (keeping up-to-date)

CHAPTER 2
Acquire and Allocate Resources

Once you've investigated what resources are available for digital marketing, and have reported on which ones are needed, the next step is to kit the organisation out for the digital age.

However it's important to keep in mind that not every item will be a brand new product requiring research, a written report and approval before the organisation can make use of it. Many purchases will be for things the organisation already has, including subscription renewals, filling empty stock, arranging routine maintenance and updating superseded technology and devices.

Purchasing Physical Resources

Some resources and tools can be purchased online, some will need to be purchased at a store and some may need quotes and input from several suppliers.

Purchasing Methods

However you plan to pay for new resources, there will be purchasing procedures in place within the company. Here are some typical examples of the way businesses choose to pay for the various costs it accrues when conducting business both on- and offline.

Buy Outright – This method simply involves the organisation paying the total amount of a product or service, leaving no outstanding amount.

Bulk Purchasing – Purchasing in bulk enables a company to secure low prices by placing substantial orders. Although bulk purchasing offers price advantages, it is not always the best purchasing method to use if you do not need large quantities of every product you purchase.

Bidding/Tender – The organisation invites vendors and suppliers to provide quotes or cost forecasts and then it chooses among the available options.

Barter – Barter is a type of purchasing method that involves exchanging products or services other than cash for supplies and materials. The process of bartering can expand your purchasing power because it generally costs less to produce an item than the retail value on which you base your bartering arrangement.

Contract Hire – Sometimes an organisation may require casual/temporary staff to be employed on contract for a finite period. This may also apply to hiring tangible resources like devices or even vehicles which are serviced according to a flat hourly charge.

Hire – Organisations can hire items they only need temporarily, or on a long-term basis. It's a cost-effective option for organisations that are just starting out to equip their office with electronics and office equipment.

Outsourcing – Yes, more and more businesses are turning over parts of their operations to outside experts, allowing owners to focus on critical needs and growth.

Petty Cash – Petty cash is a purchasing method appropriate for small, 'band-aid' purchases, such as paper clips, that you have forgotten to include in your office supply order.

In large organisations it is mostly the case that social media managers will need to get approval before they can go ahead and purchase online resources. Quite often this will mean they will need to identify the resource, justify its purchase and prove why the specific company or brand of resource is the best for the organisations' needs. This persuasion process has been discussed earlier in the book.

Traditionally, when a purchase needed to be made, an organisation would generate a purchase order form and then send it out to the relevant supplier. Once the supplier provided the product, the organisation would receive an invoice to pay for the item/s.

As is the case with most processes, online purchasing has streamlined this process as can be seen in the infographic:

TRADITIONAL BUYING

Purchase order → Receive items → Pay for item/s

NEW BUYING

Purchase order → Pay for item/s → Receive item/s

Ensuring Quality and Quantity

In the past, when ordered items came in to an organisation, someone was responsible for checking the correct quantity had been delivered and that they were of acceptable quality. This was generally the purchasing department who, once the order was assessed, would arrange for payment to be made.

In the new realm, where payment is made before receiving the product, this control process can sometimes be forgotten.

Use a Checklist

It's important that each and every organisation does the research before committing to online purchases and, once they're bought, check that these resources are worth their price tags.

Try implementing a checklist to make sure each purchase is based on the same criteria. This checklist should also contain the name and title of the person who is requesting the item be bought. This will mean online resource acquisition will be easily tracked and monitored.

Here's a template checklist to use when buying online resources and checking their quality:

Checking the resource's authority:

- Does the resource have a reputable organisation or expert behind it?

- Check the author's credentials and affiliation. Is the author an expert in the field?

- Are the sources of information stated? Can you verify the information?

- Can the author be contacted for clarification?

- Check for organisational or author biases.

Checking for relevance:

- Is the material at this site useful, unique, accurate or is it derivative, repetitious, or doubtful?

- Is the purpose of the resource clearly stated? Does it fulfil its purpose?

- What items are included in the resource? What subject area, time period, formats or types of material are covered?

- Is the information factual or opinion?

- Does the site contain original information or simply links?

- How frequently is the resource updated?

- Does the site have clear and obvious pointers to new content?

Checking the cost and accessibility:

- Is the site available on a consistent basis?

- Is response time fast?

- Do any links lead to a dead-end?

- Is this a fee-based site? Can non-members still have access to part of the site?

- Must you register a name and password before using the site?

Maintaining Resources and Keeping Up-To-Date

In order to keep abreast of which items need to be purchased, maintained or replaced and when, certain tasks can be assigned to different employees who can be held accountable for maintaining specific business resources on an ongoing basis.

Information about which resources the company has and who is responsible for each item will need to be tracked efficiently.

Maintaining Online Resources

Because online resources are not necessarily tangible things, it is easy to lose track of them! If a subscription is forgotten or social media advertising is not monitored, the organisation's business accounts could still be getting charged or access to a valuable online resource could get cut off. To make sure there is no wastage and all online resources are up to date, you can make use of your default diary or content calendar

You'll need to record the following:

- Each resource currently being paid for.

- Which staff members make use of it.

- How much it costs.

- How often it needs to be renewed.

- The dates of each renewal.

It also helps to constantly have your eye out for new products that perform the same functions. Follow blogs and do your research to make sure you've got the best (and possibly cheapest) resource for the job.

Maintaining Offline Resources

When it comes to keeping track of the organisation's offline resources – devices, furniture, vehicles, etc. – an asset register needs to be implemented. Organisations use such registers to keep a record of all existing assets, to add new assets as they are acquired and to remove previous assets that have been disposed of.

An asset register fulfils a number of purposes:

- To calculate the total value of all assets.

- To locate assets if they are used in different areas.

- To maintain a security register against theft.

- To know when to update old assets.

- To keep track of who uses each asset.

- To earmark unused assets.

Prompt Allocation of Resources

Many resources cannot be implemented and allocated the moment they have been purchased. Quite often these resources will need trained individuals manning them in order to be effective and efficient, so organisations must remember that time is another potential cost of implementing new resources.

This stage needs to be planned for because production can be disrupted if staff do not promptly receive all the resources they need to function. Prompt allocation means income for the organisation.

Training and education about these resources can also be time-consuming activities. In the case of some online resources, tutorial webinar-style videos that take 10 minutes to watch are common. In other cases it may take hours or days to learn how to operate a certain program, app or device.

Consultation on Allocation

Consultation with individuals and teams on the allocation of resources is positive and participative when conducted using appropriate interpersonal skills.

When consulting with various staff and managers about the organisation's social media and digital marketing implementation requirements it's important all parties feel they can contribute to the discussion/s.

Good people skills will go a long way when investigating what is needed because in some cases the allocation of resources can be an emotive issue. Not all departments receive or need precisely the same amount or level of access to all the resources available. Departments may be required to demonstrate why they need certain devices or tools more than others in the organisation.

There is always a limit to what the organisation can provide for its work teams and in situations like negotiating who gets what, discussing shortfalls and/or investigating resource wastage, well developed interpersonal skills can:

- Reduce friction in the workplace.

- Increase efficiency and productivity.

- Reduce management time spent dealing with issues arising from conflict.

- Increase employee morale.

- Reduce mistakes, need for rework and complaints.

- Increase company revenue.

A well-developed set of interpersonal skills is demonstrated in the following ways:

Being an 'active listener' – Let your peers speak and listen to what they are saying, even if you don't agree. When they are finished talking, take a breath before you start to speak; this will show them you don't just want to talk over the top and that you've absorbed what they've said.

Using appropriate body language – Avoid negative or aggressive gestures like crossed arms. Make sure to smile where appropriate, stand tall and make eye contact.

Inviting input from individuals – You may need to seek out the opinions of those in the organisation who may be too shy to stand in front of a group or senior management. Introverts mustn't be lost in the crowd.

Speaking clearly with articulate language – Be inclusive of everyone in the organisation as some may have impairments or language barriers.

Keeping everyone informed – By being transparent in your intentions, people will understand what the organisation's objectives are and contribute relevant information.

Being humorous and optimistic – It's not all business. Having a laugh and expressing positive views is contagious. Just remember to keep it appropriate i.e. no jokes at the expense of others.

Exercising patience – Not everyone processes and understands concepts in the same way. Take the time to make sure that whomever you're talking to understands what you're saying.

END OF CHAPTER ACTIVITY – Acquire and Allocate Resources

1. Develop a 10-point checklist for the most common resources your business purchases on a regular basis.

CHAPTER 3
Monitor and Report on Resource Usage

In order to assess whether the resources that have been purchased for the social media and digital marketing activities within the organisation have been advantageous, you need to return to your original marketing aims and objectives.

Aims and objectives are the benchmarks set in order to gauge and improve market share. Clearly defining these from the beginning is the best way to stay on track and define very quickly what does and doesn't work for the organisation.

Measuring ROI in Social Media

In social media there are a number of ways to monitor and measure return on investment (ROI) in these platforms. Facebook Insights and Google Analytics are two such examples.

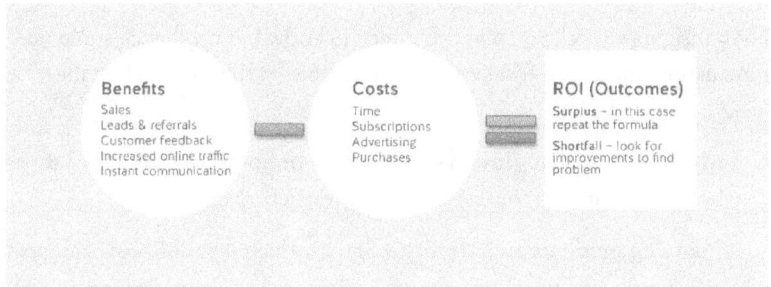

ROI Formulas

The net ROI of any campaign can only be gauged once the campaign has finished. Up until that point, the figures should be used as a guide to make sure objectives are on track for achievement. Given the mutable nature of the digital realm, you may find that part way through the campaign some objectives will need to be altered because some activities may outperform or underperform expectations.

There are four commonly used formulas to determine ROI. None of them is absolute gospel and which one you use will depend on which one your organisation will believe and value.

Formula 1: ROI: The Costs were X; the Benefits were Y

This is about offering all available information and allowing management or the client to make comparisons and assessments for themselves.

Formula 2: ROI = Benefits − Costs

Subtracting the costs from the benefits gives a simple number that will come up as a surplus or a shortfall.

Formula 3: ROI = Benefits / Costs

This will produce a ratio to indicate how much has been achieved from all of the combined costs of the activities. This is sometimes referred to as a Return on Assets and Return on Sales calculation.

Formula 4: ROI = (Benefits − Costs) / Costs

Gives a ratio using both formulas 2 and 3. This is about comparing the ultimate ROI to the costs (and not the benefits to the costs as in Formulas 2 & 3).

Using Facebook Insights to Establish Impact

Facebook Insights will tell you what you need to know but it will take some time and experimentation. Facebook Insights tracks a number of things including the following:

Monthly fan base growth − keeps track of how many "likes" your page has generated last month on the 1st day of every month.

Post engagement and virality − Shows which types of posts are most effective at keeping your fans engaged, as well as sharing your posts with their friends.

Page "like" source − Here you can see which content has generated the most likes.

Total Tab views − This will show you the number of times each of your tabs was viewed during the date range you selected.

Referring traffic sources − This will show you which websites are sending the most traffic to your Facebook fan page.

To reach your audience at the right time and day, you'll need to experiment with posting different posts here and there over different days, times and, eventually, months.

Obviously you don't want to bombard your fan base by posting continuously every hour, every day over a week to see the heavy traffic times. You'll need to spread out your posts over several weeks.

Yes, it takes time!

You'll then need to look closely at the post engagement and virality section of the Facebook Insights – which posts were most popular? Look at these popular posts and note the following data:

- Which day of the week were the best posts published – is there a pattern?

- What time of day were the best posts published – were the morning posts more successful or in the evening?

- What sorts of posts were most successful – photos, videos, question posts? Things about the behind-the-scenes operation of your organisation or references to popular culture?

You'll also need to look at the Insights to determine where your target audience resides – this will help you with determining time zones and when is best for people not living in your own time zone.

Not all posts need to go viral

Believe it or not if a post doesn't go crazy with tons of likes and comments and shares you don't need to be alarmed. Look at your timeline as a whole – each post that is published is just one piece of the puzzle. Sometimes it's easy to lose sight of the big picture – your timeline of all your posts is what visitors see when they come to your page. Yes, they may see posts individually in their news feeds but the aim is to entice them back to your timeline to look at more of your content there.

It's for this reason you need to balance your posts. Don't just post pictures. Don't just post jokes/comments/etc. Mix it up. Think about your approach to posting like you would approach to your diet: if you just ate a ham sandwich for lunch, it's unlikely you'll want it also for dinner and the following breakfast and then lunch again. Plus this isn't a very well-rounded diet.

The best way to approach this 'big picture' is to balance posts that have nothing to do with your brand (i.e. jokes or inspirational quotes) with information directly related to the organisation or products/services.

Improving Resource Use with Google

Continuous improvement is the concept that organisations need to continually review their operations. The marketplace is ever-changing nowadays so resource planning and consulting the right parties is something that needs to be done more regularly than ever before.

Given that people now search for practically everything online – products, services, events, etc. – better use of Google and keywords in particular will maximise the return on your online resources.

In order to position your brand prominently using social media and digital marketing you need to consult the right sources and collect feedback regularly. In this case it's worth looking to Google Keywords. The textual content on your site and your profiles play a big part in SEO. Think: what keywords would your target audience use to find you?

As an example, if you had a website for a ski resort, you shouldn't simply target the keywords "ski" or "snowboard." These terms are far too general and will have a ton of competing sites.

You're targeting people who want to go skiing. When a term is too general, you will have visitors who are looking for anything related to skiing and snowboarding, not visitors specifically looking to go on a skiing holiday. People who are looking to go skiing are not typing those keywords in the search box. The type of people who are likely to come and stay at your resort will be searching with keywords that look more like these: "ski resorts", "cheap ski holiday" or even localised terms like "Thredbo ski resorts".

You also would not optimise a web page for a single keyword. For example, "doctor" – with all the specialised areas in the medical industry you'd want to target people searching for specific doctors, specific surgery locations or specific health problems.

Make way for keywords

It's a waste of time to optimise your site and your social media profiles for keywords that nobody searches for, and this is where Google Keywords comes in. Once you have an idea of some of the keywords you think apply to your organisation, the next step is to gain feedback on which of these trends highest.

Once you've got your keywords and worked out which ones will work best, it's time to write them into the text of your site and profiles. The more times you feature each one, the more hits you have for the Google and other search engine spiders to pick up and run with.

You should choose keywords based on quality over quantity. That's because more relevant keywords are likely to give you better results – keywords with higher search traffic or more advertiser competition don't necessarily provide more qualified leads.

Learn how to use the Keyword Tool.

- Sign in to your AdWords account at https://adwords.google.com

- Click the Tools and Analysis drop-down menu and select Keyword Tool.

- Enter a word or phrase, or a website's address, in the different sections of the box.

- Click Search. Your results will appear in the table.

Maintain Good Resource Records

You've likely invested a lot in various equipment and resource purchases and part of understanding their impact is to keep records – in accordance with your organisational requirements, of course.

Paperwork isn't exciting but it is paramount for every organisation. Some of the types of records organisations need to keep track of include:

- Subscriptions to online resources.

- Industry-group membership information.

- Email databases.

- Supplier lists and alternative sources for items.

- Invoices.

- Stock levels.

- Quotes.

- Facebook Insight reports.

- Google Analytic report.

- Reports from third party sites on various online tolls and their performance.

'Going paperless'

The digital era has given birth to the concept of 'going paperless'. According to Wikipedia, a paperless office is a work environment in which the use of paper is eliminated or greatly reduced. Going paperless can save money, boost productivity, save space, make documentation and information sharing easier, keep personal information more secure, and help the environment.

The concept can also be extended to communications that go outside of the office.

As long as the system is set up and kept up-to-date, computerised resource and stock management can provide real-time data on every aspect of your organisation at the click of a button.

Instigating the process to eliminate paper in any organisation is a journey and all employees need to be dedicated to the process. For example, finding solutions to replace regular printing from computers. Some records that are already archived in hard copy cannot, obviously, be destroyed until they are out of date unless the organisation arranges to have them scanned and recorded electronically. So the paperless process may take up to several years to take effect in any organisation.

Cloud systems – Cloud computing systems are great enablers of paperless record keeping. A cloud is a place where documentation can be archived confidentially on a server hosting the information away from the organisation's location. Generally these clouds host data in more than one location thus guaranteeing users will never lose their data be it due to system failure, natural disasters, acts of God, etc.

Most organisations pay a fee or subscription to place its records with cloud computing systems. Large multinational organisations may even build their own cloud systems.

In the case of companies creating a lot of data and records, traditional data collection and archiving may be necessary like external hard drives which are updated regularly and stored in an alternative location to the office space itself.

END OF CHAPTER ACTIVITY – Monitor and Report on Resource Usage

1. Start a document for your keywords that can be updated and adapted as your goals change. That way if you are stuck for a blog idea you have a source of inspiration.

2. Develop a measurement strategy to assess and monitor the effectiveness of social media and digital marketing activities including reputation management, against actual cost to identify shortfalls or surpluses.

Conclusion

Good resource management may not be the sexiest part of dealing with social media or running your online business, but it is fundamental to your success.

By now, you should appreciate that it is critical to know:

- What resources are available to your organisation in the way of social media and digital marketing.

- Which parties to consult about resources both in-house and external to the organisation.

- What avenues for advertising are available online.

- How to construct a report for requesting resources and identifying areas of need.

- The methods you can use to pay for various resources.

- How to calculate the ROI of various resources and identify which ones work for your organisation and which don't.

- How to maximise your SEO.

All of this activity needs to be recorded and monitored for maximum efficiency. You can sell the best products in the world or offer the best customer service but if you don't look after the back-of-house paperwork money will go down the drain being wasted on unnecessary purchases, subscriptions and even staff hours. And that's the last thing any business owner wants.

If you would like to sign up to my monthly newsletter with tips and tricks, head to my website www.lisaharrison.com.au.

Lisa Harrison

www.ingramcontent.com/pod-product-compliance
Lightning Source LLC
Chambersburg PA
CBHW071013180526
45168CB00003B/1399